Dea sister Dee

Glitter
in the
Dust

DAN M. KHANNA

You are a glitter —

Dan Kha

ISBN: 069280272
ISBN-13: 978-0692802724

DEDICATION

This book is dedicated to the two mentors in my life:

Mr. Rasik Shah and Dr. Otto Butz.

They believed in me, encouraged me and guided me at the right time towards the right path. They referred to me as a phoenix, who rises from the ashes. I am eternally grateful to them. My life has been blessed by their presence.

God bless them.

CONTENTS

MAKE A HARD HEART

Hearts are fragile
Delicate and sensitive
Easy to hurt
Always wanting what it can't get
Always ready for the next
Thrust of hurt
Would it be nice
If a heart was hard
No emotions
A piece of stone
That stays the same
No matter what happens
But, then
It won't be a heart
A solid residue
Of a life
So what if it is still a heart.

HOMELESS WITH A HOME

I have a home
But I am homeless
I have a home
But it is empty
I visit relatives (family)
But I am shut out
There is no place for me
In their homes
It is their home
And they have moved on
I visit loved ones
But their door is shut
I knock and knock
But their door is shut
I knock and knock
The door remains shut
Telling me
It is no longer my home
It does not belong here.

There are new occupants
To this hone.
I visit friends
But their rooms
Are occupied
By other friends
New and latest
I am now
A forgotten soul
A memory that
Must be forgotten
I wander home to home
And then return
To my home
And relax in its solitude
I am reflecting
I am homeless
In my home.

2

LIVING IN A DARK BOX

The dark box
Where I pass
My wasted life
Is fragile
The stained cardboard
Beaten
By rain, wind and sun
Is my home
A place of shelter
Where I exist
Surrounded by
Empty darkness
No windows, no doors
A place to reflect
On life and my life
As the box gets carried away
And dropped in the garbage.

AN ALIEN IN MY OWN PLANET

I stare at the faces
That walk the streets
Of our planet
I don't recognize them
They don't look familiar
They are all different
Aliens with no faces
No values
Greedy eyes
Shunning you
Hinting, why are you here?
You don't belong here
You have integrity, values, beliefs
Convictions, hope, faith, ambition
You are definitely not part of this world
Show me, clearly telling me
I don't belong here
I am alien in my own planet.

STANDING IN THE DUST

The caravan
Has passed me by
Horses and carriage
Spread dirt and dust
I stand alone
Waving my hand
Wondering
Why it didn't stop for me?
Why it ignored me?
Now I stand
With my baggage
When the next caravan will come
But until then
I stand and wait
In a dust storm
Hope and faith
My only diversion.

LAUGHING AT LIFE

I laugh at life
For what it has
Done to me
Life laughs at me
For what I have
Done to myself
We both laugh
At each other
The sense of humor
Makes living easy
No tears of laughter
Streak down our faces
Dripping on lips
With their salty taste
Awakening feelings
Of joy and sorrow
As our laughter continues.

LAUGHING AT LIFE (2)

I laugh at life
For what it has made me
Life laughs at me
For what I have become
We both laugh
At each other
For we are
Two of a kind
Both not knowing
How to live
Enjoying our follies and mistakes
Sharing the blunders
With a sense of humor
For that is all we have
To ease the pain
As we journey together
To our end
Full of laughter and joy.

LAUGHING AT DEATH

It was a dream
Or was it?
A knock, a jolt
An angelic figure
Beckoning me
I ask
    It is your time
    Death awaits you
I laughed
Is it a joke?
    No, I am here to take you
You got to be kidding
I still have dreams
    But, you had your chances
    And you blew it
So, what
It was my life
I did what I did
Right or wrong
Good or bad
You cannot change that
    But I can end
    It all for you
    Take you to a place
    Where you can
    Argue as much as you want
But, I don't want to argue
I want to live
And take my time
To decide
When I want to go
    You can't
    For I determine
    When you go
But who are you?
You just showed up
But, who are you?

You just showed up
At your whim
That is a joke
I don't even know you
Except that
You exist
And will come for me
Some day
It is okay
But I am not ready
I have
Visions of the future
That you
Cannot take away
So go away
      But, I can't
      For it is my duty
      To bring you
Why me?
      It was your turn
Who said it?
      Time
But, time never ends
It is perpetual
And I am in the middle
Of a new life
That will
Tell the world
That I was here
I made an impact
I left a legacy
So, leave me alone
For I need time
      I can't give you that
      Time may be perpetual
      But not for mortals
      You are mortal
      Just a speck
      In the dust
      No one will know

You ever existed
Or ceased to exist
I don't care
About anybody
It is me I have to live with
That is all that matters
I will go
When I am ready
So, leave me
Before I start laughing at you.

VICTIM OF SELF

I was born innocent
Everything was fun
Everyone was equal
Then I grew up
Learning from society
Dismantling the mask
Of innocence
For a new face of
Biases and prejudice
Changing one mask
For another
I lost myself
In this wilderness of life
Lost my innocence
I was
A victim of self.

EXIST TO DIE

Why do we exist?
To die for some
As Robert Browning, the poet, said,
    "Grow old along with me
    The last of life
    For which the first
    Was made."
And he was right
We exist for death
We do our song and dance
Perform for the world audience
And then the curtain falls
The final curtain
with no encore
The show is over
Time to call
It an end.

DREAMS ARE DREAMS

There are dreams
And there are dreams
There are dreams
That we yearn for
And there are dreams
That remain dreams
There are dreams
That come to us
While we are asleep
Howling through our subconscious
Into vivid images
Of space and time
That vanish
When we wake
Dreams are not reality
They are visions of a world
That we may not see
They are just dreams.

THE IMPERFECT LOVE

The beauty of life
Is that
It is so imperfect
The beauty lies
In its imperfections
In its unpredictabilities
In its vulnerabilities
For love has its wants
Its desires
But it does not know
How to achieve it
It flounders
In the ocean of expectations
Awakening reclamation
From stone walls
As it pounds
Our empty hopes
Not giving up
For love never gives up
It is a heart beat
That goes on
Until life ceases
Love is a heartbeat
That keeps on pounding
Until it finds a life
That it can live through
To a new world
Where it will meet love
Another love
To embrace life
For love and life
Are imperfect souls
Both wanting each other
But both eluding each other.

LUCKY TO LOVE

I would rather love
And lose
Than not love at all
Love is a divine gift
The feelings, the emotions
Make you alive
Make you feel
That you are
In the heart of God
In His bosom
Feeling
The highest form of expression
Feeling
That you are alive
Alive with love
And you can last
Through eternity.

THE DARK SIDE OF ME

We all have a dark side
I have mine too
In anger and frustration
I may think evil of some people
I may think life is unfair
I may not feel sympathy for some
I may feel that some people
Don't deserve good lives
I may feel that
Some evils get unpunished
But the dark side
Lasts a short time
The thoughts pass
Then I am back
To my normal self
Good and bad
A human.

THE END OF FLOW

I had a muse
I had ideas
The thoughts were flowing
Through the ink
Onto paper
Burning at things
Of the mind
Into unforgettable memories
As the ink dries up
The paper is blank
The writings stop
Life comes to a standstill
Having exhausted
All creativity
To live a life
Without words on a paper
A blank page
The end of flow.

SADDLING TWO HORSES

I ride two horses
At the same time
One of dreams
One of reality
It is dangerous
I perch precariously
Uncertain stability
Ready for a fall
A great fall
For dreams and reality
Never merge
Like two horses
My ride will always be dangerous
It is a ride that I must make
To reach
Where I must
For dreams to become a reality.

PATTERN TO THIS MADNESS

There is a pattern
To this madness
That I call life
My life
I live in a mad world
Among mad people
Where madness is normal
To the point
That my madness
Is now part of my life
Making mistakes
At every step of my life
For all the wrong reasons
But I am consistent
My madness is persistent
It is constant
It is there
A great pattern.

LOST HORIZONS

There is a world
I envision
A Shangri-La
Where a utopian world
Holds a perfect life
Where humanity is revered
Integrity worshipped
Love cherished
Friendship valued
It is a world
Across horizons
In the mountains
Away from
Dying societies
That self-destructed
In deceit and greed
Void of compassion
And snow-filled peaks
That watered
The fertile lands
Is barren
The heat has dried
All vegetation and life
Become wasteland
That once held
Fertile lives
Now stand desolate
Ravished by the
Greed of humanity
Plundering life
That sustains it
Disappearing horizons
Of hope
Until we are left
Alone and cold
No hope in sight.

IT IS JUST A GAME

It is just a game
Life
Sometimes you win
Sometimes you lose
Sometimes you just break even
Life should not
Be taken seriously
For we participate in it
Unwittingly and unwillingly
We are thrown in it
Like dice
We take our chances
We take risks
The dice
Determine our fate
All we can do is throw
If the dice are fair
They will decide our fate
But if the dice are tainted
They will control our fate
We don't know
What dice we will get
Fair or tainted
That itself is a game
A game in a game
We are pawns
That move with the dice
And we accept our fate
What gets through at us
We catch, we miss
The game goes on
And we must accept
That life is
Just a game.

RELIC OF THE PAST

Ancient virtues
Remnant values of the past
Treasures in dungeons
Beauty in antiques
Scars of wisdom
Washing of the wind
Carvings of nature
That is me
A relic of the past
That believes in value, integrity, beauty
In an unholy world
Inhabited by vacant souls
That walk around
As lifeless ghosts
Trying to imitate
Humans that have faded
Into oblivion
As I remain
A remnant of the past.

EMPTY VALUES AROUND

Values
Our honest beliefs
That give us dignity and individuality
Values and respect
To trust
Compassion for humans
Honesty in relationships
Is being eroded
And left behind
In the dust
People talk of values
As if they were commodities
For sale at cheap stores
Not knowing
That values are never sold
It is an inner virtue
That is the basis
Of all humankind
That is soundly ignored
Distorted by society
To save their own interest
Lying and deceit
Broken promises
Walking over people
Now is accepted as a norm
That we accept casually
For we are part of it
Why have values in society
When we don't have values
It is too much of a burden
It is easy to live
In an empty world,
With empty values.

WHERE IS HOME?

Where is home
To a traveler through life
That is constantly on the move
Searching for a place
Where he can rest in peace
And die with dignity
It is not a home
Where one lives
It is not a home
With a glamorous structure
It is not a home
Surrounded by relatives and friends
It is not a home
That gives you shelter
From heat and cold
It is not a home
Where you socialize and entertain
It is not a home
That protects you from the outside world
For the outside world is in shambles
In need of protection from itself
The home is
Where your heart is
Where you feel free and liberated
Where your energy is at its peak
Where creativity blossoms
Where the world seems tranquil
Where people are warm
Welcoming you as an individual
Is there such a place?
Is there such a home?
So I must continue
My journey to find
My true home.

EVERYONE FOR SALE

We get excited by
The sale signs
We love bargains
Even though we know
That sales are illusions
Attractions to spend our lives
For illusionary bargains
But it is not just
The goods or services for sale
People are for sale
There is always a price
For which we will sell ourselves
Our values, principles, dignity
For our safety or survival
For we must live
To leave a mark
Even a mark of disdain
There is a price
For which we will sell
Look at the politicians
Lawyers and public officials
Media and stars
Family and friends
Selling to save their souls
For materialistic existence
Even though
The soul is divine
It is not part of this shallow life
But we sell our souls
For instant gratification
For short term pleasures
In the end
We are all whores
Except, whores give pleasure
We don't.

FREEDOM TO DIE

Death is inevitable
It comes to us all
It is the only certainty
A "must" event for all of us
It comes
When it comes
So why not
Have
The freedom to die
Not avoid death
But to enjoy it
And die with dignity and class
In my own way
There is one choice
One freedom
That I must
Do it my way
At least die
The way I want
In pleasure
Savoring every last minute
Enjoying my life
With favorite foods and drinks
Music and books
Still growing intellectually
As life ebbs out of you
The divine luck
Slowly grinds your body and soul
To a halt
With dignity and grace
As you breathe
The last air of a decaying world
To leave on your terms
To end it with dignity
And your freedom.

FREEDOM FROM LIFE

Life is a cruel prison
That holds you until you die
Whether you are guilty or not
Because it thrives
On your helplessness
You are stuck with it
You are its cherished victim
To suck and bleed
Until you are dry and devoid
And then it throws you
To the vultures
To feed on you
Until not a remnant
Is left of you
Just a faded memory
Of a life
In need of freedom.

VICTIMS OF OUR CHILDREN

Our children
Are born through us
But are they our flesh and blood?
In a sense, yes
But, they are not our minds
Their minds are of a future
That we do not see
For that is not our world
We are of
Two different worlds
Though we are parents
Think that ours is the same world
But it is not
Our children
Are not our children anymore
They have moved on
While we are left behind
Victims of hope
That they will b like us
They will respect us
They will love us
That is an illusion
For we must realize
We are not them
We are not like them
We belong to a world
That died when we had our children
Soon they will leave
To start their nests
We are left alone
Starting the empty nest
The nest that we made for our children
Is now empty
Time to fly
For we are now
Victims of our children.

THE SYSTEM

The system
Is an organism
That feeds upon itself
For its survival
Creating mechanisms
To shield itself
With rules and regulations
That shout out outsiders and change
For change is a threat to a system
It wants status quo
Politics or public
Academic or non-profit
As organizations became systems
Organisms
Betraying their original goals
For survival
It is now just becoming a system
With its own rules and regulations
A living organism.

THE REPUBLIC

The republic, the state
Corrupt at the top
Rotten to the core
Using and exploiting
Its simple people
With lies and insecurities
Is a regime
That will meet its fate
At the last dust of lost societies
That imploded, self-destructed
To preserve the victors
Who served themselves
Not the people
For people are to be exploited
For their survival
The Machiavellian model
People are expendable.

THE POWER OF PEOPLE

The power of people
Is important
They are brainwashed
By politicians, by media
Manipulated, seduced
Because people are wanton
They don't read
Their knowledge is diminishing
They are exploited
For their ignorance
Divide and conquer
The power of the people
Is no more
Just an illusion
At the whims of the ruler or ruling class
Preying on ignorant people
Making promises they do not believe

THE CRUELTIES OF HUMANS

The cruelties
That humans inflict
On other humans
Is unbelievable
Indiscriminate killing
Mental and physical abuse
Callousness and neglect
Abandonment of responsibilities
Self-service and selfishness
Walking over each other
Ignoring compassion
Breeding in greed and avarice
Hurting children and elders
Where did we learn this
Not from God
But from other humans
Shallow and weak
We are evil.

THE AFTERLIFE

There is a world
That is waiting for me
At the other side of the universe
Where I will be truly me
A real person
I was supposed to be
In this life
A person I betrayed
I became a person
Prone to mistakes
Living shallow life
The afterlife
Is my redemption
To recover and recoup
My soul
That abandoned me
I searched
For meaning
In a desolate life
Shedding all my values
To exist in a carnal world
But, the afterlife
Is my home
To gain some respect
Within myself
To live a life
That I was supposed to live
A life
That will tell me
Who I am really
A person
Of substance.

A GOOD MAN

I am a good man
At least that is what I think
A good man in my eyes
Or a good man
In the eyes of others
But, then
What is "good"?
The fine line
Between good and bad
Is blurring
Depends on how
And who looks at it
I was born good
Pure and innocent
And then I grew up
In a polluted and corrupted world
Where survival and greed
Are the values
Of existence
As I struggle
To come out alive
From the grave
That I have dug for myself
Without dust
Clean and clear
Washed away
By my mistakes and blunders
To look at the mirror
Of life
As I face the eternal truth
Am I a good man?
I thought I was
I think I am
But only God and destiny
Are the ultimate judges.

RETURNING TO THE FIELDS

The fields
That I grew up in
Were full of life
Nature and nurture
Providing me
With all the ingredients
To live a rich life
The smell, aroma, food
Lush with water and flowers
I was part of it
It was part of me
We were one
A life in tune with nature
But then I left the field
To seek paths
In wilderness
And rugged mountains
I got lost
I stumbled
I got hurt
But I kept going
Searching for the fields
That I had abandoned
I yearned for soft earth
The gentle touch of nature
I want to return
To the fields
Where I can live
In open air
And be one again
At peace with nature
To embrace
The fields
Of my life.

THE LAST OF THE HUMANS

The humans
The endangered species
About to become extinct
Due to its own follies
Blunders and greed
Filling the environment
That sustains it
For instant pleasures
And self-gratification
Selling their souls
For greed and money
Where have all the humans gone?
Into an empty space of survival
Selling values, beliefs, integrity
Themselves
For a price
That is cheap
To anyone who will buy
Until there is nothing to sell
Just an empty shell
That is useless
Of no value
Then wonder
Who am I?
Stripped of all dignity
All divine gifts
Just a carcass
Of flesh and bones
That is wasting
To rot and decay
A feast of the vultures
The species
That came with a promise
Now nearing extinction
Destroyed by self
The last of the humans.

DREAMS OF A SOCIETY

A society
That is full of hope and dreams
Love and peace
Remains a dream
The utopian empire
Has crashed many times
As we struggle
To carve and existence
In a decaying world
Destroyed by hatred
While we still introduce
New humans
Into a dying world
Hoping that a
New society of perfection
Will emerge
Just to see our
Dreams crashing
As we continue
To give birth and kill
Hoping and failing
Dreams of a society
That fails to emerge
While we slowly
Fade into oblivion
And the dreams
Of a society
Just remain a dream.

DREAMING OF A RAINBOW

The rainbow
Spreading across the universe
Sparkling its brilliant colors
Across the sky
Inviting dreams and hopes
Of a dying life
Staring at a rainbow
That is just a mirage
At the mercy of
Sun and rain
Hoping that clouds
Don't cover the sky
And kill the dream
As the rainbow
Disappears
To be replaced
By an illusion of hope.

UNFIT TO LIVE

We live
We die
Some live better
Some live bad
Some are privileged
Some are not
And then there are those
Who are unfit to live
For they make mistakes
From the day they are born
And continue to do so
Throughout their lives
Piling one on top of another
Until the pile becomes a mountain
That crushes them
These are the people
Who are unfit to live
Unfit not because
They are born humans
Unfit because
Divine guidance is not with them
Luck deserted them at birth
Humanity trampled them
These are the people
Who are unfit to live
And to them
Life is a burden
That must be cast off
As soon as possible
To end the pain and agony
Of life
That is not worth living
For we are, I am,
Unfit to live.

THE HUMAN TOUCH

Humans have a touch
That destroys civilizations
Killing their own kind
For pleasure and greed
But, then
They don't stop at their own kind
They plunder
The earth
That gives them life
For they think
That their lives are limited
So they want to limit
Every nature's life
They kill rocks
 They kill plants
They cut through
Mountains and jungles
Destroying in their paths
In the name of progress
But more for their
Selfish pursuits
Of their short lives' gratification
Ignoring the earth
That gives sustenance
For they think
They own the earth
Not realizing
That they are useless against nature
They are vulnerable
They are useless
So, show humility
Let your touch be gentle
With respect
Make a human touch
A divine touch.

THE PATIENCE OF NATURE

Nature
Defines time
In its own terms
Nurturing it with patience
Creating rhythms and cycles
That move the world
As it carves
The earth
In its own vision
Creating mountains and oceans
Valleys and rivers
Color and shape
Slowly dripping
Gradually planting
Life and beauty
Into a desolate dangerous world
Hope that we will learn
From its caring patience
But, we humans
Live for a short time
For instant gratification
Making patience
Into a new virtue
As we come and go
While nature stops
Living through eternity
Specks of life
Forgotten and scattered
In the hands
Of nature.

MY MIND'S MIND

My mind
Has a mind of its own
It does not listen to me
It ignores me
It avoids me
It treats me with contempt
Brushing me aside
And making decisions
Without me in mind
It was not like that
I was in control
I learned, educated myself
Acquired knowledge
Nurtured my mind
Let it expand
Let it think
And then
It deserted me
It was too good for me
It made decisions
That hurt me
It made choices
That led me astray
Once we were one
Now we are aliens
To function without my mind
Floundering and existing
As my mind
Waved at me
From a distance
Bidding me goodbye
As I am left to
Fend off love without my mind
Just alone.

SUM TOTAL OF LIFE

As I tally
My assets and liabilities
Trying to determine
If I was profitable
Or a loss
I would be happy
To just break even
For I came from nothing
And will go into nothing
The assets I piled
Turned into liability
As they get
Fully depreciated
With no value left
And I was left
Without resources
As I fell into bankruptcy
And closed my life.

THE HUMAN ANIMAL

The human
Is an animal
With instincts for survival
Killing and stealing
To prolong life
But a human
Is an advanced animal
While an animal
Strives on basic survival
Humans rationalized
Survival by greed and lies
Killing for pleasure
Just to advance its case
Hollow as it might be
For the air of superiority
Permeates its being
For it can kill
Animals with weapons
Not with hands
For it is too weak
And the human
Is not even a noble animal
For animals serve a purpose
While humans
Exist for exploitation
Feeling superior
Just like the dinosaurs
Until nature
Can't stand it
And wipe the planet
Of humans
Making it pure and natural
Hoping a new species
Will emerge
That will make earth
A better place.

THE LAST OF THE BREED

I was bred
To respect people
Hold certain values
Follow principles
That uphold truth
Trust fellow people
And develop integrity
That is unquestioned
Learn and grow
For knowledge is power
And never ends
And that was my breeding
Given to me
By my parents,
Bless their souls,
Now I stand
Alone
In an empty village
Which is devoid of people
Who have left the town
In search of selfishness, greed and avarice
Shedding all goodness
That was ingrained in them
As they ride out
Storming dust in my eyes
Left alone
Reflecting on my bred
Lonely and alone
Wondering what happened
It was good
While it lasted
The last of the bred
That believed in something
That belief in life
Is worth living.

THE REMAINING DAYS

As I count
The remaining days
Of my wasted life
I wonder
When will it all end
How many days are left
What do I need to do
In my remaining days
Reflect on my past
Cry over my follies
Admire my achievements
Or just let it go
For I have lived
I cannot undo the past
It is over
The future -
Is a remnant of my past.

DREAMS OF A MAN

I had dreams
Of a wonderful home
Full of fun and family
Excitement vibrating through
Every pore
And then nature
Decaying the structure
Until it collapses in a heap
I stand alone
Pounded by rain and sun
Seeking shelter
In plants and fields
Scattering dreams
Sheltering illusions
Until reality sets in
And then
All I see
Is a hut
In the distance
A quiet place
Strong and silent
A place
Beckoning me
To give me solace
And peace
That eluded me
All my life
And now that hut
Is my home
A simple place
Where I can be at peace
And rest
Until the end beckons me.

WALKING IN, WALKING OUT

The curtain call
Time to enter
The stage.
Face the audience
Do my skit
Will they love it?
Will they detest it?
I don't know.
I enter the stage
Greeted with applause
For they have not seen
My performance yet
I respond
Just like a puppet
I sing and dance
Soliloquy and monologue
Crying and laughing
To the amusement
Of the audience
I get applauded
I get booed
But the show must go on
My performance ends
I have uttered
My last dialogue
It is over
I walk off the stage
Quietly and down
My game is over
Forgotten
As I unmask and wash
The artificial makeup
From my face
To be just me
Love's artist.

RISE FROM THE ASHES

The ashes
Scattered and scared
Gathered in the dust
Trying to carve
A life
Out of dead remnants
Igniting fires
Out of sparks
That burst into an eruption
To live and prolong
Life that died some time ago
But life does not die
The ashes are the skin
That must be discarded
For life to emerge
From its cocoon
To rise from its ashes.

THE FINAL FLAME

As the flame dies
It bursts into brightness
Emitting a myriad of colors
That announce its demise
Its final battle
Against life
As it loses its grip
But still fighting
To leave a message
That it won't die in vain
Even in its end moments
It will ignite the world
Brighten it up
For the last time
Before it plunges
Into eternal darkness
The final flame.

UNSHACKLING RESPONSIBILITIES

The end is near
The boat is heavy
I must lighten up
Unshackle the responsibilities
That I have carried
All my life
Bent with the burdens
I must straighten up
To be able to walk
Through the gates
Erect and proud
That I fulfilled my responsibilities
I am free
Of obligations
My conscious is clear
As I stand above the clouds
In full freedom.

MY LIFE IN THIS WORLD

My life in this world
Is full of contradictions
It keeps me alive
While it pushes me
Towards my demise
It gives me hope
Then it shatters my dreams
It soars to great achievements
Then crashes ferociously
It loves me
It hates me
It pleases me
It berates me
It amuses me
But, it is my life
I am in love with it
I will die within in.

THE HOME IS A PRISON

My home is my castle
Heavily stoned
That surrounds me
Keeps me warm
Protects me from the outside
While I breathe its stale air
I am comfortable
That is what I think
I am safe
That is what I believe
I am there
Because that is what
I believe is my home
But my home
Is also my prison
A self-imposed prison
That gives me a false sense of security
By keeping me inside
Shutting me off
From the outside world
In an artificial world
Of likes and dislikes
That are far from reality
But it is a home
A place of my own
Good and bad
A place where I belong
In my world
That is untouched by light and dust
Pure and simple
Far away from reality
But a place
That I must rest
A quiet prison.

RETURNING TO THE TRENCHES

I have wandered long enough
Searching for purpose
That still eludes me
I have climbed the mountains
Marched through the valleys
Still I remain
Where I started
Travelling all over
But remaining still
I must stay still
Stop the journey
Between the trenches
To regroup
To rethink
And start my journey again
With new hope and directions
Diving into a sunset of my choosing.

MISFIT TO THE END

I knew when I was born
That I was a misfit
In this world
Whether I was wrong for the world
Or whether the world was wrong for me
Maybe, I was born
In the wrong time
But me and life
May have known better times
But I continue to exist
Out of sync with the world
But never one with the world
And as my time
Draws to a close
I will leave it
Misfit to the end
From start to finish.

A PERFECT LIFE IN AN IMPERFECT WORLD

I live a perfect life
Full of mistakes and misjudgments
Gaining and losing opportunities
Just like a regular life
But it does not bother me
For I live in an imperfect world
Where my imperfections seem perfect
A world without values
Rampant competition and greed
Seeming normal
Accepted by the people is part of life
For we are as corrupt
As our leaders
So we are alright
Imperfection breeds imperfection
But I am alright
From imperfect
Perfect for an imperfect world.

LIFE OF A LONELY SURVIVOR

I have survived
A lonely life
In a miserable world
That exchanges values and principles
For hollowness and shallowness
To live a life
Of simple virtues and responsibilities
That means all of us
But, it is survival
That is proud
It had beliefs
It grew and learned
Even if it was lonely
It was worth it
For a lonely survivor.

MOTION OF SURVIVAL

The day starts
With an alarm
Nudging me
To face the world
Like any other day
The cycle of life
That continues
In perpetual motion
Killing time
Until sunset
Another day passed
Another day survived
As I rest thinking
What did I do this day
What did I accomplish
I stare at blankness
Ready to take on another day.

THE FINAL PAGES

The book is ending
But I do not know
The ending
A few pages are left
So what should I write?
A happy ending
A sad ending
Or, just a mystery
Of how life may end
And leave it to imagination
The final pages
Are the sum total of the book
What will it be?
Will it bomb?
But the pages
Are carved in stone
So, let it be
A memorable end.

IN SEARCH OF LIFE

I started my journey
At birth
In search of life
And as I near the sunset
I still search
I still haven't found it
It keeps eluding me
Maybe the life I seek
Does not exist
Maybe the life that exists
I do not want
We keeping missing each other
Like two trains
Passing each other in the night
Acknowledging each other
With a whistle
But never meeting
Just like the parallel
Tracks of the train
For if they meet
The train derails
So we travel
On distant tracks
Acknowledging and waving
Whistling and whimpering
Knowing that both are there
Apart but together
Existing but not together
Still searching for each other
And the search goes on
Until the day
When I find it
In eternity.

MY BLINDNESS

There was a time
When I could see everything
From near to distance
Left or right
Up or down
My eyes saw things
That others ignored
I had a clear view of the world
And I prided myself
That I was in touch with the world
What I saw
I could touch
Then came a night
A haunting night
When lightening stuck me
As I lay in a turbulent sleep
Awakening me with a jolt
I stood erect
I reached out
To touch
But my hands
Fell on empty spaces
People, places and images
Eluded me
My vision was tainted
I could only see
Part of life
Half of my life
Just disappeared
In a stroke
As I grope
To grasp things
I cannot see
Bumping into things
That should not be in my way
Waving to people
That I cannot see

Hoping they are there
Adjusting to life
In half a world
Forcing me to
Desert my territory
For unknown spaces
Where my blindness won't matter
Where I will not bump into things
Where my half world
Will be a full world
Looking at the world
With imperfect vision
Making an imperfect world
Look perfect
Keeping total imperfections
Away from me
As I continue
To hit unknown targets
Trying to live
A normal life
In a blind world
Then I realize
I am not blind
I am just fractured and defective
But still perfect
For a world
That is decaying from top to bottom
It is not me that is blind
It is the world
For I acknowledge my deformities
But the world goes on
Ignoring its frailties
Why blindness
Is a blessing.

THE CONTRADICTIONS OF LIFE

Every aspect of life
Is a contradiction
We are here
Why we don't know
We are born to parents
We don't choose
We hope life will be good
We walk toward it
Not knowing if it will happen
We love, we marry
Not knowing if it will work
We keep falling in and out of love
We are happy and sad
At the same time
Hope and disillusionment
Every aspect of life
Is a contradiction
It is just a life.

DREAMS OF A VAGRANT

Even vagrants have dreams
Eve wanderers have dreams
Even homeless men have dreams
For dreams are the only right
Of a human that is unique to him
The only thing
That he can call his own
A wish, a hope
Whether it happens
Does not matter
For it propels them
Toward a world
That they want
A world full of happiness
A world of honesty
A world of love and peace
For dreams are just dreams
Hope and faith
In the great goodness of mankind
That remains an illusion
But dreams
Are the spirit of survival
An elixir of life
A whirl of illusions
We cannot give in
Even as a vagrant
For in the true sense
We are all vagrants
Searching for meaning
In a meaningless life
Passing through
Dreams are the only hope
That keeps us alive
And searching for the truth.

THERE WAS A TIME

There was a time
When I thought
I was good
I controlled my life
I knew where I was going
I saw my future
My dreams were fulfilled
And I lived a happy
Healthy life
And destined to die a natural death
Surrounded by family and friends
Adoring and missing me
My lovers saddened and crying
It was a thought
A belief
That I aspired
It was a time
A time now lost
A time that does not exist
My future is uncertain
I am alone
Abandoned and alone
Shrinking beliefs
Lost lovers
A simple existence
With hope and expectations
Of a life
That I did not achieve
In this life
But it was a good time
A time, I thought
Was my own.

THE SLOW MASSACRE

Life ebbs slowly
Eroding each faculty
One by one
Diminishing desires and hopes
As it chips away
At our bodies
Slowing as
Pounding us
Until we get
Used to its blows
And gradually succumb to it
In sweet pain
Finding pleasure
In erosion
As we enter
A state of bliss and purity
The sweetness of a slow massacre.

UNSHACKLING MEMORIES

Memories are part of us
Whether they hold us back
Or propel us forward
Depends on how we deal with them
Unshackling memories is not easy
They are embedded in us
Haunting us in our dreams
Taunting us in our actions
Driving us to undesirable locations
Propelling us into space
Either to throw us into
A different orbit
Or let us crash
Vigorously to earth
Memories can be blessings
Or hindrance
But, it is best
To unshackle memories
That hinder you
For the past is over
It can never come back
Unless you allow it
For the future awaits you
That is where you belong
In a world
Where you create new memories
Memories that are pleasurable
Positive and peaceful
For you live in a world
That is yours
Uniquely yours
A world for you
For your future.

THE ANCHOR OF THE PAST

The past is an anchor
That holds us still
For that is safe and settled
While the waves of the ocean
Undulate beneath us
Wanting us to move
With the flow of nature
But the anchor holds firm
For it has its own
Score to settle
It thrives on firmness and control
That is its strength
But an anchor is just an anchor
A relic of the past
Whose job is to hold
According to the laws of nature
It must be severed
The anklet
That this anchor is
To our feet
Must be cut
Otherwise
It will pull us
Down into the ocean
Drowning us with memories of the past
That have lost significance
As we lay dormant
At the bottom of the ocean
Unless we break free
And let us flow with nature
To our destined lands
A future of our dreams.

THE COLLAPSING MONUMENTS

The fabric of our society
Is crumbling
The foundations
Of our institutions
That were built on
Values, freedom and hope
Are being eroded
By greed, corruption and incompetence
As we stare
Blindly and blatantly
At our collapsing monuments
Watching the decay with empathy
Helpless and ignorant
Warped by the
Onslaught of deceit and lies
Hurled at us
By our leaders and media
The corruption of corporations
Driven by greed
For short-term justification
At the cost of our
Long-term institutions of liberty
Eroding opportunities
Except for selected few
Who exploit the system
To preserve the few
While our monuments collapse
We just keep staring at it
Until all is left
Is a rubble of dust
That carries memories of a past society
That crumbled like
Many other great societies of the past
History repeats
And we never learn.

SERIES OF CHALLENGES

My life has been a series of challenges
That are thrown my way
By divine forces
Family, friends and society
I try to jump over obstacles
Like a runner over a hurdle
Trying to aim the jump
Over the wall
Sometimes clearing it
Sometimes bumping against it
Sometimes just falling
As I set to
Continue the race
The race of life
For which I was not prepared
Not coached or warned
As I struggle towards
The next hurdle
Just relying on my instinct
Guts and faith
As I crash
Through each challenge
One by one
Hoping that
It will be the last challenge
But life is not that kind
Challenges are interwoven into life
And I must unravel them
One at a time
Until there are no more challenges left
Just a straight race
Boring and straight
As I long for
The arrows of challenges.

THE FINGER OF FATE

I hold the finger of fate
As it guides me through life
Pointing me in unknown directions
Gently nudging me
To try alone
But I am afraid
To let go
For the few times
I did let go
I stumbled into unchartered waters
Where I was bruised and pounded
By invisible forces
Leaving me not dead but alive
Enough life
To recoup
And get up
To face another onslaught
Of life
But this time
I hold the finger of fate
And not letting it go
Trusting my life
To its will
For my schemes
Never worked
Now I hope
It will guide me
To my dreams
As I hold onto its finger
Tightly and gently
As I am led
Somewhere, some place
Where my destiny
Awaits me.

DECLINING

There was a time
When it was hard and erect
Ready to go places
Wherever there was a soft opening
Shimmering thrusts
Elating in its eruptions
Resting peacefully
And then ready to take on the world
It was a good life
Fun, joy and play
As it ages
And reflects
On its many adventures
It wonders
Was it worth it?
Wasting so much energy
On deserted terrains
Sowing seeds
On brown lands
Until the well
Grew empty
Drawing water
Became a chore
Holding pride
Diminishes
Not necessarily by choice
But life
The natural cycle
That cannot remain
On top forever
Men are devastated
Unnatural endowments
Play short-term tricks
Until you realize
It is over
And fun while it lasted.

SEARCHING

I am in search
Of life that continues
To elude me
I am in search of a world
Where there is peace and tranquility
And people live in peace and contentment
I am in search of a partner
That values me as a friend
And brings out the best in me
I am in search of friends
That accept me for who I am
Pushing me in the right direction with gentleness
I am in search of family
That is not overbearing and critical
Creating a nurturing environment for growth
I am in search of children
Who do not need me for their own purpose
Rather than respect me for what I did for them
I am in search of colleagues
Who value collaboration
Rather than snapping and back-biting
I am in search of service
That value you a virtuous
Rather than a necessary evil
For their growth and profit
I am in search of leaders
Who extol integrity and values
Rather than exploitation and manipulation
But, I am still searching
There has to be a place
Where one is at
Peace with oneself
In harmony with nature
Friendship with all
And so I embark
Searching.

AN ANCIENT MARINER

There was once
An ancient mariner
Who roamed the seas
In his dependable old boat
Visiting places and sights
On whim and impulse
Guided by instinct and guts
Experiencing life
With passion and excitement
Making friends with unknown souls
Sharing thoughts and feelings with strangers
As his boat
Flew over undulating waters
Propelled and pummeled
In all directions
It was a free world
Everything near
But nothing in sight
Just a floating journey
Searching for an abyss
That takes you
Into a new world
Whether it exists
The mariner did not know
He had faith
And enjoyed the journey
It didn't matter where it led
But it was an adventure
Of a free spirit
A journey we all should take
To be free from constraints
Just letting
Life, nature and destiny
Exist with each other.

GOING THROUGH THE MOTIONS

The sun rises
I wake up
I reflect on the upcoming day
Same routine
Survive to kill time
Going through the motions
Of living
But not living
Just existing
To kill time
And wait for the inevitable
The burdens of the past
The mistaken adventures
Have squeezed all life
Out of life
As each day becomes a burden
A load I must carry
To shed on the last day of life
The will to live
Dissipating with each day
Wondering how hopes
How dreams
Vanished into twilight
As I stand
Deserted and stranded
On a long terrain
Waiting for the vultures
Circling with anticipation
At my fall
To feast upon
A body
That outlived itself.

DEEPLY IN DEBT

I stare at my dwindling paycheck
Deep beneath the pile of debt
That surrounds me
The credit cards, the loans
With their hidden charges
Declining below
My income every month
The random offers of loans
To encourage more debt
The love of instant gratification
The seduction of material goods
Creating an illusion of happiness
That lives month to month
While we struggle
To get out of debt.

TO SPARK A DEAD LIFE

I lay in my coffin
The lid about to be closed
And piles of dust ready
To engulf me
But, I am not dead
I still have
Things to do
Dreams to fulfill
Adventures to sail
Challenges to overcome
I need a spark
To give life
To the dead
To become alive
And do all things
That I need to do
There is still time
I need a spark.

GOD'S OUSTSOURCING

Some time ago
Somewhere in the heavens
When God was about to make me
He decided it was too much trouble
But I was in the list to be made
So God decided
That my making should be
Outsourced
To cheap contractors
Who may do
An adequate job
On average people
For a fraction of the time
So, here I am
A defective individual
With faults and dents
Trying to carve an existence
From a imperfect world
Maybe my imperfections
Fit our world
Making mistakes
That are part of life
Body going through illnesses
As it streams toward its end
With creaking sounds
And frequent repairs
A cheap product
Of mass production
One of many
That will never amount to
Anything special
But to just fill a void
In a landscape of humanity
With imperfections of cheap labor
Of God's outsourcing.

GOD'S WARRANTY

When I was made
And sold to Earth
I came with a limited
Manufacturer's warranty
I performed well
In initial stages
I could walk and exist
And go through the motions
Of living
As I was programmed to do
But as my psyche
Aged
My body creaked
My mind slowed
I had to fend for myself
As my warranty had expired
I was on my own
Fixing myself
With screws and bandages
Trying to hold myself
Together in a tumbling world
I wish I had asked for
An extended warranty
To get Divine repair
Whenever I broke
Rather than taking myself
To crackpot repairmen
When God was self-indulgent
So now I am on my own
Repairing myself as much as possible
Avoiding repair garages
Longing for
Divine intervention
And a chance
To extend my warranty.

SO MUCH LOST, SO LITTLE TIME

As Robert Frost said,
    "The woods are lovely dark and deep
    And, have promises to keep
    And miles to go before I sleep."

I ponder at the sunset of my life
Surrounded by uncertainty and unfulfillment
Preparing for the end
But, not ready for the end
For I have unfulfilled dreams
That keep haunting me
Reminding me
That it is not over
I may have lost a lot
Maybe everything
But not myself
My hopes, dreams and faith
The end beckons me
With passion
Chastising me for my complacency
Reminding me
That my destiny
Is not over
My end will not come
Until I do
What I was sent to do
Leave a legacy
Of my thoughts
As I journeyed through life times
Capturing all
In the remaining time
And I have to promise
To me that my left
Is just the beginning
I have all the time in the world.

THE LIFE WRECKER

Is there an award
For people to wreck their own lives?
I will win it every time
For I am a master of it
I have done it too many times
In every aspect of my life
I have mastered the act
Not that I am dumb
Not that I am uneducated
Not that I have no knowledge
But it is just my brain
That seems to rationalize
Everything I do
Even turning absurdity
Into a reality
Telling me
That what I am doing
Is perfectly right
Shutting me away from reality
And plunging me
Into a box
That keeps me hidden
From what I should have done
I keep doing this
I build my mounting success
Then invite a wrecking ball
To slam into the structure
Grinding it into dust
As I search for sanity
Among the broken pieces
Ready to build
Another to wreck
I am the greatest
Life wrecker.

WHAT SHOULD I DO WITH ME?

Every morning
I look in the mirror
And see a faulty person
With cracks and imperfections
And now I wonder
What should I do with me?
I have choices
I can continue to live as I have
I can wait for my end
And accept the usual defects
I can change my course
To leave a legacy of my existence
Or just continue to stare
Every morning
Into the cracked mirror
I am confused
I do not know what to do
Accepting the blows of fate
As I get pummeled into the ground
Getting stronger with each blow
Building character
In a lifeless soul
To take on the challenges
That I will confront in the future
Is that I should do?
Face the future with dignity
And carve a world
That is my own
My own creation
Of love, happiness and contentment
That is my destiny.

A FAULTY STRUCTURE

I am built
On a faulty structure
With cracks in its foundation
And holes in its walls
That makes it
A dangerous architecture
About to collapse at any time
Just held together
By sheer will
To stand erect
As earthquakes shake it
Storms pound it
Termites gnaw at it
Hoping that the structure
Will become
An ancient monument
That will be admired
In due time
For its history of endurance
And resistance to natural laws
As it fought invaders
From within and without
Trying to leave a legacy
That time will appreciate
And admire a structure
For its ancient beauty
And carvings of time
And stories of a beautiful world
That once existed within its walls
Rich tapestries and loving stories
That once adorned it
With joyful music and culture
Now just a memory
Just a structure.

HURTING MYSELF

I am very good
At hurting myself
I think I owe it to me
I am sure
I have the right
Why let anyone outside hurt me
When I can do a great job
On me
I am my own worst enemy
Devastating my career
Blowing my relationships
Devouring my body
Messing up my dreams
Wasting opportunity after opportunity
I am my best enemy
I deserve an award
For doing an outstanding job
Of hurting myself.

THE TRAVELER'S JOURNEY NEVER ENDS

I left my home
Many years ago
On an unknown journey
That will take me
Over continents
Deserts and oceans
Over the mountains
To places I ha never seen
Meeting strangers who became friends
Finding relationships
That brought joy and sorrow
Enriching me
With knowledge about our world
Understanding people
I liked and disliked
Growing intellectually
On an unending
Quest for wisdom
And questions about the universe
That keep running away from me
And remaining unanswered
I look for hope
In desolate places
For in Divine guidance
As I walk paths
With no directions
That lead nowhere
Just a path
That continues my journey
To unknown places
In search of destiny
That will forever
Elude me.

ABOUT THE AUTHOR

Dan Khanna considers himself a traveler through life enjoying an adventurous journey. Dan was born in New Delhi, India. After he completed high school, at St. Columbus High School, Dan left India striking out for California via short stays in London, Montreal and Milwaukee, Wisconsin. Although his dream was to pursue a career in the arts, acting, music, and writing, a quirk of fate placed him in engineering college and pursuing a business management career, in which he excelled. Dan completed an undergraduate program in engineering, and a Master and Doctorate in Business Administration.

Dan worked in Silicon Valley's high technology firms and was a CEO and founder of several firms. He changed careers to be a professor. Now, he again is pursuing his dream in creative endeavors.

Dan is the quintessential Renaissance Man, whose interests span the gamut of the arts, sciences, history, social and political studies, classics and philosophy. His search for knowledge began in his early life where his father was the Chief Education Officer of Delhi and his mother was a Sanskrit scholar. Dan speaks English, Hindi, Urdu, Punjabi, and Gujarati.

As a child, Dan read voraciously, particularly enjoying novels, such as Sherlock Holmes, Agatha Christie, Earl Stanley Gardener, Ian Fleming's James Bond series and classic works of Shakespeare, Tolstoy, Dickens, Oscar Wilde, Thomas Hardy, and other writers. He was very interested in poetry and read English poems of Browning, Keats, Milton, Tennyson, and Frost, as well as, other poets, while mastering Urdu poetry. His intellectual interests including studying Western and Eastern philosophers, especially Socrates, from whom he learned questioning methodology employed in his research, lectures and seminars.

During his parochial education, Dan was interested in various sports: cricket, soccer and field hockey. His love for the arts and music was honed to a level that he performed in plays, movies and solo concerts.

Dan's present journey is devoted to creative arts and activities, primarily writing poetry, fiction and non-fiction books and plays, while continuing to acquire knowledge of diverse subjects. He has published one book and has written over twelve hundred poems. Dan has several non-fiction and fiction books in development.

Proof

Made in the USA
Charleston, SC
11 December 2016